MARINE CORPS

Simon Rose

AV² provides enriched content that supplements and complements this book. Weigl's AV² books strive to create inspired learning and engage young minds in a total learning experience.

Your AV² Media Enhanced books come alive with...

 Audio
Listen to sections of the book read aloud.

 Key Words
Study vocabulary, and complete a matching word activity.

 Video
Watch informative video clips.

 Quizzes
Test your knowledge.

 Embedded Weblinks
Gain additional information for research.

 Slide Show
View images and captions, and prepare a presentation.

 Try This!
Complete activities and hands-on experiments.

... and much, much more!

Go to **www.av2books.com**, and enter this book's unique code.

BOOK CODE

U 2 4 2 6 1 0

AV² by Weigl brings you media enhanced books that support active learning.

Published by AV² by Weigl
350 5th Avenue, 59th Floor
New York, NY 10118
Website: www.av2books.com   www.weigl.com

Library of Congress Cataloging-in-Publication Data
Rose, Simon, 1961- Marine Corps / Simon Rose.
     p. cm. -- (U.S. Armed Forces)
 Includes index.
 Audience: Grades 4 to 6.
 ISBN 978-1-61913-294-8 (hbk. : alk. paper) -- ISBN 978-1-61913-298-6 (pbk. : alk. paper)
 1. United States. Marine Corps--Juvenile literature. I. Title. VE23.R67 2013
 359.9'60973--dc23

                        2012021996

Printed in the United States of America in North Mankato, Minnesota
1 2 3 4 5 6 7 8 9 16 15 14 13 12

062012
WEP170512

Project Coordinator: Aaron Carr
Design: Mandy Christiansen

CONTENTS

WHAT IS THE MARINE CORPS?

The Marine Corps is one of the main branches of the United States Armed Forces. The other branches are the Army, the Navy, the Air Force, and the Coast Guard. The Marine Corps is the main **amphibious** force of the United States military. This means it is made up of forces that work on both land and water. The Marines have a close relationship with the Navy, and they work with Navy forces during training.

The Marine Corps is part of the Department of Defense. This department is in charge of all branches of the Armed Forces except the Coast Guard. The secretary of defense is the head of this department. The president of the United States is commander-in-chief of the entire Armed Forces. The Marine Corps has more than 200,000 Marines on full-time duty and about 40,000 part-time Marine Reserves.

★ The Marine Corps works on both land and water. It leads U.S. military attacks on enemy forces along seacoasts.

STRUCTURE OF THE U.S. ARMED FORCES

- Air Force
- Army
- Marine Corps
- Navy
- Coast Guard

- Special Reaction Team
- Scout Snipers
- Force Recon

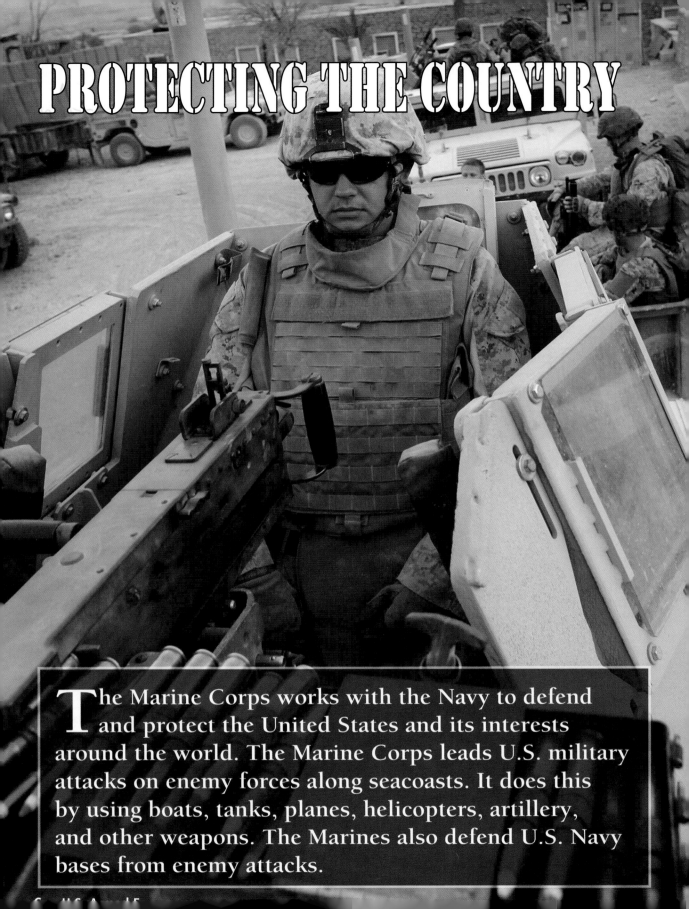

PROTECTING THE COUNTRY

The Marine Corps works with the Navy to defend and protect the United States and its interests around the world. The Marine Corps leads U.S. military attacks on enemy forces along seacoasts. It does this by using boats, tanks, planes, helicopters, artillery, and other weapons. The Marines also defend U.S. Navy bases from enemy attacks.

The U.S. Marine Corps Reserve supports the Marine Corps. The Marine Reserve has more than 180 training centers throughout the United States. Reserves receive the same training as regular Marines. They can be called upon to quickly report for active duty in wartime or during a national emergency.

On the Front Lines

On the battlefield, the Marine Corps is in charge of all amphibious operations. Marines travel on Navy ships, planes, or helicopters and then fight the enemy on land. The Air Force and the Army sometime join the fight. When the battle is over, the Marines may be involved in **humanitarian activities**.

THE MARINES' HYMN

The Marines' Hymn is the official song of the U.S. Marine Corps. These are the first four lines of the song. The "Halls of Montezuma" refers to Marine involvement in the Mexican-American War, and the "shores of Tripoli" to the First Barbary War.

From the Halls of Montezuma to the shores of Tripoli,

We fight our country's battles, in the air, on land, and sea,

First to fight for right and freedom and to keep our honor clean,

We are proud to claim the title of United States Marine.

HISTORY OF THE MARINES

The **Continental Congress** founded the Marines on November 10, 1775, during the American Revolutionary War. They were called the **Continental Marines** then. This force broke up after the war ended in 1783, but it was set up again in 1798. Since then, the U.S. Marine Corps has taken part in every armed conflict that the United States has been involved in.

1783
★ Victory over Great Britain in the American Revolution

1861 TO 1865
★ American Civil War

1899 TO 1901
★ Boxer Rebellion in China

1775
★ Marines are formed

1812
★ The War of 1812 against Great Britain begins

1776
★ The Declaration of Independence is signed

1846 TO 1848
★ Mexican-American War

1898
★ Spanish-American War

1801 TO 1805
★ First Barbary War against pirates in Africa

1801

1846

The Marine Corps is mainly an amphibious force, but it sometimes fights far inland. Marines battled in the forests of northern France during World War I. Today, they fight in the desert in Afghanistan. A famous photograph shows Marines raising the U.S. flag after defeating Japan in the Battle of Iwo Jima. This photo was used as the model for the Marine Corps War Memorial statue at Arlington National Cemetery near Washington, DC.

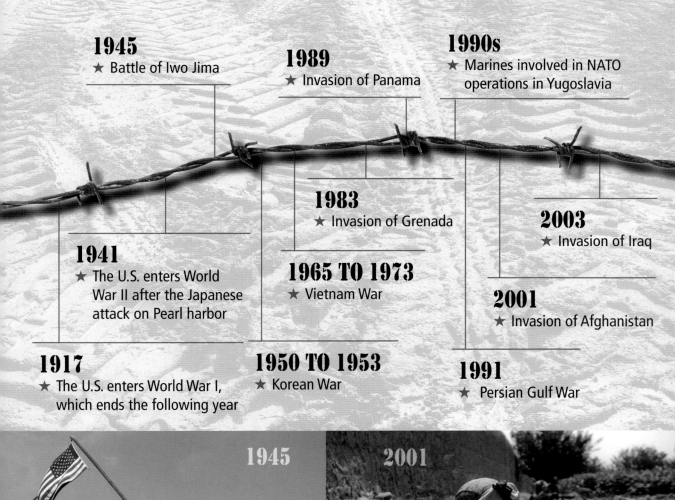

1945
★ Battle of Iwo Jima

1989
★ Invasion of Panama

1990s
★ Marines involved in NATO operations in Yugoslavia

1983
★ Invasion of Grenada

2003
★ Invasion of Iraq

1941
★ The U.S. enters World War II after the Japanese attack on Pearl harbor

1965 TO 1973
★ Vietnam War

2001
★ Invasion of Afghanistan

1917
★ The U.S. enters World War I, which ends the following year

1950 TO 1953
★ Korean War

1991
★ Persian Gulf War

1945

2001

U.S. MARINE BASES AROUND THE WORLD

The U.S. Marine Corps currently has 15 bases in the United States. The Marines also operate bases in other countries, including Afghanistan, Cuba, Djibouti, Germany, Japan, and South Korea.

1 California

Camp Pendleton is the main Marine base in the western United States. It is located in southern California. The base was set up in 1942 to train Marines to serve in World War II. It is home to the 1st Marine Division. Other branches of the Armed Services also train at the camp. The base is part of a military community of more than 36,000 people. This includes members of the military and their families.

2 North Carolina

Camp Lejeune is the main Marine training facility in the eastern United States. It is located along the coast of North Carolina. The base has 14 miles of beaches. This makes it a perfect site for amphibious combat training. The base is named after Lieutenant General John Lejeune, who served as the 13th Commandant of the Marine Corps. He is sometimes referred to as "the greatest of all Leathernecks."

3

Germany
The United States Marine Corps Forces Europe is based at Panzerkaserne Barracks in Boblingen, Germany. The Marine Corps Forces Europe is part of the United States European Command, which is in charge of all U.S. military operations in Europe.

4

Afghanistan
There are several Marine bases in Afghanistan. Most Marines in Afghanistan are based at Camp Leatherneck. There are more than 20,000 Marines and civilians on this base. It is located in Helmand Province in southern Afghanistan.

5

Japan
The Marines operate a number of bases in Japan. Most Marines in Japan belong to the III Marine Expeditionary Force, which is based at Camp Courtney. This base is located on the island of Okinawa. It is named for Major Henry Courtney, who was killed in the Battle of Okinawa in 1945.

ARCTIC OCEAN

ASIA

EUROPE

AFRICA

INDIAN OCEAN

PACIFIC OCEAN

AUSTRALIA

MARINE UNIFORMS

The United States Marine Corps has used many different uniforms throughout its history.

THE AMERICAN REVOLUTION

Officers wore a two-cornered hat with a knot of ribbons on the side. Other Marines wore a round hat with the brim turned up on one side.

The shirt and trousers were usually white. Most officers and horsemen wore boots, while other Marines wore shoes.

WORLD WAR II

During World War II, the Marine combat uniform was made of heavy cotton material and was dull green in color with **camouflage** patterns. The jacket had a pocket on the left chest and two at the hips. It also had three metal buttons down the front.

The Marines wore a green coat with white cuffs, lapels, and lining. The coat also had a high leather collar to protect the neck against slashes from enemy swords. This is why Marines were nicknamed "Leathernecks." The modern Marine dress uniform still has a high collar.

The M1 helmet was made of steel and weighed 2.2 pounds (1 kilogram). It protected the wearer from **shrapnel**, but it did not stop bullets. A cloth with a camouflage pattern covered the helmet.

TODAY

The peaked hat is white and has a black visor.

Combat
The Marine combat uniform consists of a long shirt and trousers with a camouflage pattern, a green undershirt, and tan-colored boots. There are different camouflage patterns for different locations and seasons. The desert/summer pattern is tan, brown, and gray, and the woodland/winter pattern is mostly black, brown, and green. Marines also wear a Modular Tactical Vest that protects them from bullets and shrapnel.

Dress Blues
The best-known uniform worn by Marines today is the blue dress uniform. It is often referred to as Dress Blues. This uniform has a long-sleeved, dark-blue coat with a high collar. Officers wear a dark blue belt, while enlisted Marines wear a white belt. Medals are worn on the left side of the chest, and ribbons on the right.

Officers wear dark-blue trousers with a red stripe down the sides. Enlisted Marines wear light-blue trousers. Women may wear skirts instead of slacks.

MARINE WEAPONS

The American Revolution

The most important weapon of the American Revolution was the flintlock musket. It was a **smoothbore** gun that fired a single shot. Then it had to be reloaded. Bullets were loaded into the top end of the gun, called the muzzle. Pulling the trigger caused a piece of flint to make a spark in the gun. This ignited gunpowder and fired the bullet. The musket had a range of less than 100 yards (91 meters). This meant that men had to be very close to each other during a battle. A **bayonet** was usually attached to the musket.

Mexican-American War

Most Marines in this war used the Model 1816 Musket. This was a single-shot, muzzle-loaded flintlock gun with a 3.5-foot (1 m) long barrel. It had a range of 100 to 200 yards (91 to 183 m). The musket could be fitted with a 16-inch (40.5 centimeter) long bayonet. Some Marines used a Model 1842 Musket, a later version of the Model 1816.

World War I

The M1917 Browning Machine Gun was one of the most important weapons used by Marines in World War I. It was a heavy gun that operated on gas. When the trigger was pulled and held, bullets moved into the gun and were fired continuously by **recoil** action. The empty shells were ejected from the firing chamber automatically. This machine gun had a range of about 1,500 yards (1,372 m). It was often mounted on jeeps or other vehicles.

World War II

The M1 Garand **semiautomatic** rifle was the basic weapon used by Marines in the war. Each time the trigger was pulled, it fired a round of bullets. It then ejected the clip holding the bullets. It had a range of 500 yards (457 m). Many Marines were armed with the Thompson **submachine** gun, better known as the Tommy Gun. They also used the bazooka, a gun that fired a small rocket. The gun rested on the shoulder when it was fired. It was used against enemy tanks. The flamethrower was another important weapon in the war. Marines used this weapon against enemy forces in caves and bunkers. The flamethrower user needed to be within 10 to 15 yards (9 to 14 m) of the target, making this a dangerous job. Marines bombarded the enemy with rifle and machine-gun fire until the flamethrower user was close enough to attack.

M39 Enhanced Marksman Rifle

Today

The M4 Carbine rifle is one of the main guns used by Marines today. It is a shorter and lighter version of another widely used gun, the M16 assault rifle. The M4 is a semiautomatic gun that operates on gas. Its barrel is 14.5 inches (39.3 cm) long. The short barrel allows soldiers to use the rifle better in tight spaces. The gun has a range of 650 yards (594 m). Expert sharpshooters and snipers use the M39 Enhanced Marksman Rifle. It is more powerful than the M4 and has a greater range. When Marine snipers need even more power and longer range, they use the high-powered M107 rifle.

M107 rifle

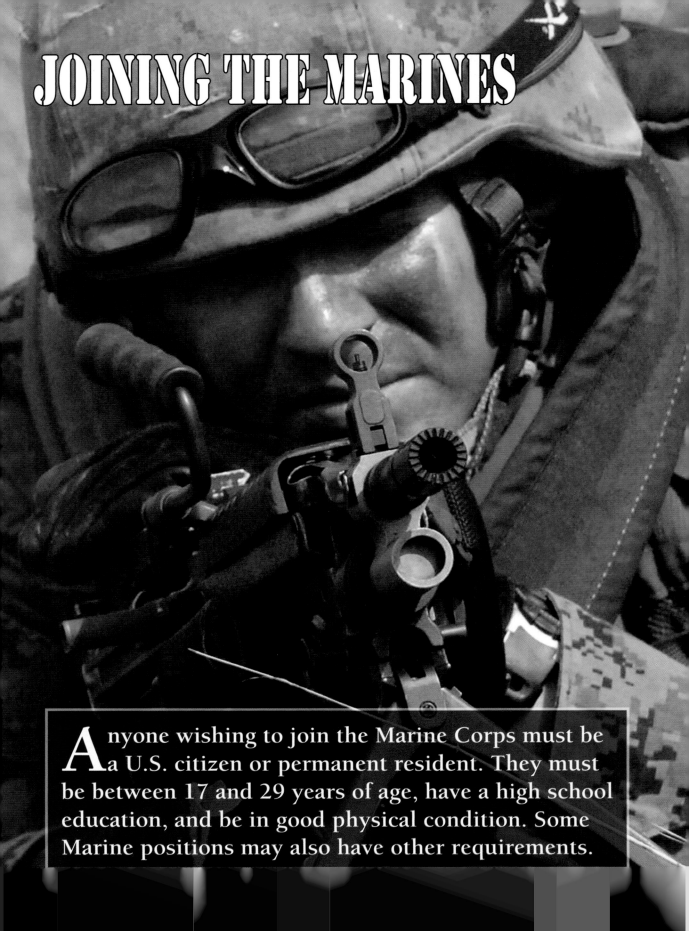

JOINING THE MARINES

Anyone wishing to join the Marine Corps must be a U.S. citizen or permanent resident. They must be between 17 and 29 years of age, have a high school education, and be in good physical condition. Some Marine positions may also have other requirements.

Applying to the Marine Corps

Step One: Talk to a recruiter

Step Two: Talk to family and friends

Step Three: Submit your application

Step Four: Visit the Military Entrance Processing Station (MEPS), where it is determined if the applicant is qualified to join the Marines

OATH OF ENLISTMENT

❝ I do solemnly swear that I will support and defend the Constitution of the United States against all enemies, foreign and domestic; that I will bear true faith and allegiance to the same; and that I will obey the orders of the President of the United States and the orders of the officers appointed over me, according to regulations and the Uniform Code of Military Justice. So help me God. ❞

Boot Camp Training for Marine Corps recruits is often called Boot Camp. It is considered the hardest recruit training in the U.S. military. The training period is 12 weeks long and consists of both educational classes and physical training. The final test for recruits is known as The Crucible. This test is 54 hours long, including 48 hours of marching. It is based on a combat situation and involves a shortage of food, lack of sleep, and many other challenges. Recruits must use all the knowledge they have gained during training to pass the test.

MARINE CORPS FACT

In 1918, Opha Mae Johnson joined the Marine Corps Reserve. She was the first woman ever to join the Marine Corps.

JOBS IN THE MARINES

Being a Marine is not just about serving in combat. There are many types of careers in the Marine Corps. There are jobs working with computers and technology, fixing military vehicles and aircraft, and keeping financial records. There are also jobs in aviation, communications, electronics, engineering, and more. Almost all jobs done by civilians are needed in the military. The training and experience gained in the Marines can lead to successful careers in civilian life after military service is completed.

Communications and Technology

Work in these areas involve the use of computers and other electronic equipment. There are jobs in computer programming, technical support, military intelligence, satellite communications, and explosives.

Business and Public Affairs

Business careers in the Marines include accounting, finance, management, and purchasing equipment and supplies. Marines in public affairs work to maintain good relationships with communications media and the general public. They may write and edit stories about the Marines for newspapers and magazines. They also may represent the Marines at community meetings and press conferences, and on television news shows.

Avionics and Construction

Jobs in avionics include installing and repairing the communications, navigation, and weapons systems of aircraft. Jobs in construction include electrical work, carpentry, and plumbing. There are also jobs operating heavy equipment, such as bulldozers and cranes.

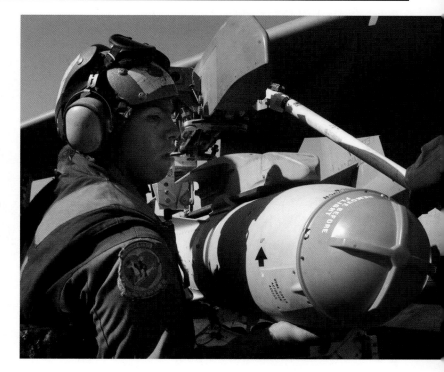

MARINE COMMUNITY LIFE

I n many ways, life in the Marine Corps is much like civilian life. Marines work regular hours at a job, they spend time with their families, and they fill their free time with hobbies, sports, or any activity they choose. Some Marines live in barracks, but others live in houses either on or off the base.

Many Marine bases have all of the facilities of most towns or cities. This may include hospitals, schools, day-care centers, libraries, sports facilities, and shopping malls. The Marine Corps has a variety of programs to improve the quality of life for families living on Marine bases. These include counseling services, programs to improve on-base education and job opportunities for family members, and programs that help families deal with the stress of having a parent working in a combat area overseas.

★ The families of some Marines live on Marine Corps bases. Many Marine bases have all the facilities of a town or city.

WRITE YOUR STORY

If you apply to join the Marine Corps, you will need to write an essay about yourself. This is also true when you apply to a college or for a job. Practice telling your story by completing this writing activity.

1 Brainstorming

Start by making notes about your interests. What are your hobbies? Do you like to read? Are you more interested in computers or power tools? Then, organize your ideas into an outline, with a clear beginning, middle, and end.

2 Writing the First Draft

A first draft does not have to be perfect. Try to get the story written. Then, read it to see if it makes sense. It will probably need revision. Even the most famous writers edit their work many times before it is completed.

3 Editing

Go through your story and remove anything that is repeated or not needed. Also, add any missing information that should be included. Be sure the text makes sense and is easy to read.

4 Proofreading

The proofreading is where you check spelling, grammar, and punctuation. During the proofread, you will often find mistakes that you missed during the editing stage. Always look for ways to make your writing the best it can be.

5 Submitting Your Story

When your text is finished, it is time to submit your story, along with any other application materials. A good essay will increase your chances of being accepted, whether it be for a school, a job, or the Marines.

TEST YOUR KNOWLEDGE

1 When were the Continental Marines founded?

2 In what year did the Battle of Iwo Jima take place?

3 What base is home to most Marines in Afghanistan?

4 What is the final test for Marine recruits?

5 What rifle is used by Marine sharpshooters and snipers?

6 What are the two main Marine bases in the United States?

7 What was the basic weapon used by Marines in World War II?

8 What is the official song of the U.S. Marine Corps?

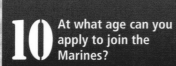
9 What is another name for the Thompson submachine gun?

10 At what age can you apply to join the Marines?

ANSWERS: 1. November 10, 1775 **2.** 1945 **3.** Camp Leatherneck **4.** The Crucible **5.** The M107 rifle **6.** Camp Pendleton and Camp Lejeune **7.** The M1 Garand semiautomatic rifle **8.** The Marines' Hymn **9.** The Tommy Gun **10.** 17 years old

KEY WORDS

amphibious: operating both on land and on water

bayonet: a knife that can be attached to the muzzle of a gun

camouflage: clothing or other items designed to blend in with the surroundings

civilian: a person who is not an active member of the armed forces

Continental Marines: name for the Marine force set up by the Continental Congress during the American Revolutionary War

humanitarian activities: efforts to save lives and prevent suffering

Marine Reserves: part-time Marines who can be called on in an emergency

military intelligence: information about the armed forces of another country

muzzle: the top end of a gun

recoil: the backward movement of a gun when it is fired

semiautomatic: a gun that can fire a round of bullets and load a new round each time the trigger is pulled

shrapnel: pieces of metal that fly out of a bullet or bomb when it explodes

smoothbore: a gun that has no grooves on the inside of the barrel

submachine gun: a lightweight automatic gun that shoots pistol-type bullets

INDEX

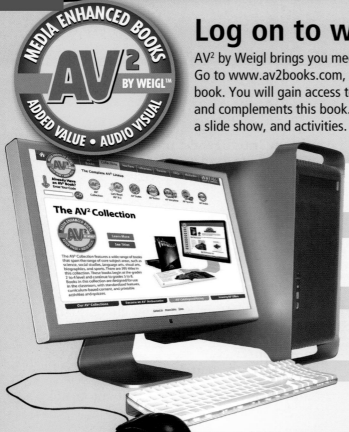

Log on to www.av2books.com

AV² by Weigl brings you media enhanced books that support active learning. Go to www.av2books.com, and enter the special code found on page 2 of this book. You will gain access to enriched and enhanced content that supplements and complements this book. Content includes video, audio, weblinks, quizzes, a slide show, and activities.

Audio
Listen to sections of the book read aloud.

Video
Watch informative video clips.

Embedded Weblinks
Gain additional information for research.

Try This!
Complete activities and hands-on experiments.

WHAT'S ONLINE?

Try This!	Embedded Weblinks	Video	**EXTRA FEATURES**
Try a timeline activity.	Read about the importance of the Marine Corps.	Watch a video about the Marine Corps.	**Audio** Listen to sections of the book read aloud.
Complete a mapping activity.	Find out more information on the history of the uniform.	Check out another video about the Marine Corps.	
Write an essay about yourself.	Learn more about Jobs in the Marine Corps.		**Key Words** Study vocabulary, and complete a matching word activity.
Test your knowledge of the Marine Corps.	Read more information about the Marine Corps.		
			Slide Show View images and captions, and prepare a presentation.
			Quizzes Test your knowledge.

AV² was built to bridge the gap between print and digital. We encourage you to tell us what you like and what you want to see in the future.

Sign up to be an AV² Ambassador at www.av2books.com/ambassador.